T0209409

From

MIDNIGHT

to

DAYLIGHT

From
MIDNIGHT
to
DAYLIGHT

The story behind the story

CHINA BLACK

FROM MIDNIGHT TO DAYLIGHT
THE STORY BEHIND THE STORY

iUniverse books may be ordered through booksellers or by contacting:

iUniverse
1663 Liberty Drive
Bloomington, IN 47403
www.iuniverse.com
844-349-9409

ISBN: 978-1-6632-4923-4 (sc)
ISBN: 978-1-6632-4927-2 (e)

Library of Congress Control Number: 2022923541

Print information available on the last page.

iUniverse rev. date: 01/04/2023

1

FROM MIDNIGHT TO DAYLIGHT.

My autobiography of life from the good and the bad and the ugly.

From Gangbanger to government

To Minister——

Going from a dark part of life in to a lighter part of life. Born in Memphis Tennessee in 1954. Having at the time one older sister.

Having my mother and father and aunts and grandmother. Never remember having a grandfather but I know it had to be one. I just can't remember him.

I can remember my grandmother, my 2 Aunt and my Aunt Living in a small house and I can remember going to church with my Grandmother with my little blue dress.

Going up a hill and there sit the church full of people and all I can remember we were there all day.

I can remember me and my sister her being two years oldest would ride this bike I snatched it from her and down the hill I went and by the time I got down the hill I seen her running after me and I foot got stuck in the wheel of the bike.

My dad have to come and free me from this bike. I remember at the age of 5 years old because I still have that same scar today. I can remember chickens running across the road and I would try to catch one of them.

I can remember my daddy saying to us that he is going to Chicago to find a job and he was offer a job and it took a week for him to go and come back to get us. Moving to Chicago going down the highways to our new life.

My dad have found a new job and an apartment on polk street on the three floor.

The house was beautiful I remember pictures hanging on the wall I remember my mother would sit us in this high chair to comb our hair.

We started off with little but we had each other this mother of mind would take some flour sugar water milk whatever else she used it would turn out to be some of the best teacakes you would eat.

This big white bowl would sit in the middle of the table and there were no limits of how much we could eat.

What a little cooking oil would do for the body specially the digestive system. I can remember on special days my daddy would put all of this girls in the car, back in does day hamburgers and French fries were 10 cents. We have the best places to eat hamburger whoopee on Roosevelt. The center park show where we would go and watch the movie.

Never paid to get into the movie we would know somebody that worked there and they would let us in the back door. I can remember when we first saw Michael Jackson and the Jackson five. Wow oh wow. We always knew that we want to see them in person and we got our chance. The even came to our school. It was a delight to have this treat every week. I would roll down the window and hang out cursing my little but off. A neighbor would asked my daddy were in that little cursing girl. I don't know where I got that cursing from but I can imagine I come from a two sided family. My mother side of the family was a little different from my dad side. You may say they were the good and the bad and the ugly. It had to be coming from some side of the family. My daddy side of the family was consider crazy. My mother side of the family were consider the nice side. My uncle and my aunt always fighting with somebody. They did unbelievable things. They didn't care what they said or did. I had one uncle that will cut you if you get in his way. I have one uncle that threw his baby brother out of a third floor window. I have a uncle that rape children. They did so many things it was scary. They started dying later in the years. This one uncle did so much dirt you would not believe how he died. Somebody took gasoline and poured on him and lit him on fire they had to have a close casket funeral. I have one uncle that had suppose too have committed suicide another uncle been stabbed to death. I can' remember any bad things about my aunt on my father side I know they were a close family and we hardly seen them. I remember my day said don't let anybody in this house we are not at home I always for some reason had a hard head. This uncle comes over to the house and I open the door and he said I am your uncle. My daddy said don't open this door. He said I wish you were not my niece. Oh my daddy was so mad. Growing up on the west side of Chicago remembering the little men that walk the street selling pepper I am a little girl and these men are the same size and I was scar so we would take off running and one day when we saw them again it was not bad at all because somebody explain to us who they were and what they did. They were making a living by selling pepper. They would go door to door. Now it was time to move again after years being in that basement it was time to go somewhere else. Our landlord was so nice and she didn't want us to move but 6 people living there it was too small. We all were growing into our teenager life. I am in school so we moved to Douglas and Lawndale. I am attending Herzl elementary I grew up as a what we call a tom boy. I just like the things boy did rolling tires, climbing trees, shooting marbles. I was a little ruff under the edges. People tried to tell me what little girls do. Jump rope, play. I love doing things the boys did because it was not that I wanted to be a boy. It was fun being a tom boy. At the tender age where I should have been playing games and studying for school work or maybe even playing with doll finding myself more and more doing bad things. It was so many things to get into and they were some good and some bad. I chose to do what I wanted to do without my parents knowing. This man we called fast walking Willie. He was about 7 foot tall. You can be running and this man would be walking and he can catch up with you. We would run like hell one day this man I seen and then I didn't see him. He was in our hallway and he tried to grab me and my cousin walk in and he ran. This man had a wife and kids he always looking for somebody for some reason or other. We always wonder what is this man trying to do. One day while we was sleeping in the living room my mother and father in their bedroom. In the dining room there was a stack of bottle against the window somehow this guy climb over these bottle and got into our house. This was away my father would try to hear somebody if they try to break in our house. This time nobody hear anything but my sister doll she was a little girl heard this man and she seen him while all of us was still sleeping ran into my father room and told him it is a man in our house we all jump up and my father got his Gun to shoot the man but the man unlock to the door and ran out the building. Today I think it was fast walking Willie. I can still see that face right now today. Come to think about it this man had to have some long legs. When I was growing up we have plenty to do we would go swimming in this statue that sit in the middle of the park. And it would pour out water we would play in it all day. I was beginning to grow a little older and no longer wanted to be a tom boy I want to be a pretty young lady now I was looking at boys my first friend I have to register for school and Dante elementary was my first school it was just me and my sister at the time.

I never like school even the first day. I remember having a little friend in my kindergarten class room we would have birthday party at school and we would have to dress up. I always wanted to be a cowgirl. I had the sweetest parents you would ever meet.

My day went out and found me this little cowgirl suit with the cowboy boots.

While my daddy would be at work I was supposed to be in school.

This little friend I had one big sister. They lived right across the street.

I wonder why her sister would come to the school to get her out of class or before we went in.

I was so close to this friend the sister would take me with them to their house. I wonder why.

I found out that her mother left for work at a certain time. After the mother go to work this is when she made her move.

I can remember her going to the bed room and stay in that room a long time and then they would come out and then I can remember her saying it is almost 3:00 and she would rush us back to school.

It was something about that clock it was always 3:00 that was the time school was out. I wonder why the teacher never question I imagine we was only in kindergarten who really know why but it happen. This was just the beginning of a trend of ditching school. We would still go out to play.

I have no clue on what and how long this went on. I know one day I went to my friend house and this day my daddy was coming to pick me and my sister up early to go shopping for new clothes.

The time the clock struck 3:00 went left her house and little late than we should have. The sister tried her best to get us back to school.

I running and here comes my dad down the street. I ran right into him. He said girl where are you coming from and he reach up in the tree and got a limb back in does day you will get a whooping with what every they can get their hands on.

It could be a shoe etc. We went home and there was no shopping I blow it. My sister got a chance to play outside but I have to look outside the window. I can remember that little small window in the bathroom. Sitting on the porch watching the kids laugh and play I try my best to get down stairs. I can see everything.

All I could do was cry. I have to stay on the porch and look at all the children playing and having fun outside. I got a chance to listen to that record the green onions. Nice summer day when all the kids in the playground jumping rope playing ball, after my daddy came home from the navy. Here come this young sailor and I look up and it was my father. We ran out in the street I can remember him driving this nice car and I remember when my sister ran in the street trying to get to my father she got hit by another car. My mother was the doctor the cook I can't see us going to the doctor I don't know if there were doctors in the 50s I know my mother got something and doctored of my sister and we she grew up she still had that scar. My dad coming home from the Navy decide it was time to move, because Sears had brought up all the land and they built stores. I didn't know any different you had to go wherever your parents went so we move on in a basement apartment.

The parties follow us. If my father and mother had a drink I didn't know about it. I can remember at the tender age of 7 this curly head man would stand by the basement store and wait until we get out of school he made sure we would have candy every day we didn't have to wait for our parent to give us anything we knew where we was going to get our money for this candy. I can remember this young man in a wheel chair he was nice looking but we didn't know why he couldn't walk and run like we could. We all was good friends. He want to like me and I didn't know what it mean he was a little older I didn't like boys we was that young. I remember the time when we got out of school and this guy was bothering us chasing us and we stop in front of this tree and a bird drop on him. Growing up in Chicago was fun and if there was any action we didn't know much about it when were kids. Never heard my mother or father talking about thing that was happen to people the way it is going on today. I remember my uncle gave me a quarter and I put in my mouth to keep my sister from knowing and I swallowed it. It was so scary but here come my mother to the rescue. She went and got some cooking grease off the stove and gave it to me and out comes the quarter. You will be surprise name was Jackie yes it was a boy name Jackie. My mother and father would have guess over there house so they would send us upstairs Jackie was the oldest and he has twin brother. Have no ideas about sex. We had all girls in our family. I guess you would say I was hot in the underwear. Putting things lightly. I had to be about 11 years of age. Moving over to the seventh grade I would say this was the age I should have been maybe twelve. Hess upper grade center. I had to dress up so I would steal my sister doll clothes she tried her best to hide them clothes but I always found them. I was snoop dog. I could find anything. One time I took her clothes and in the middle of the pants was tore and I have to pretend I didn't know what happening but she knew it was me. I stop stealing her clothes. My sister doll always kept a job. She would buy candy and would not share with us. She sit and eat a whole bag of orange slices and her lips go so big we last at her and said you need to learn how to share. I can remember going to Hess upper grade center had some of the finest I mean some good looking teacher. My favorite teacher in 8 grades was Mr. Ronald Eck. Short because I can not remember how to spell his name. Going back to 6 grade I can remember this one class mate of mind he was to fine. I went to school every day just to look at him. All my God body had their eyes on him, it was this one girl Stephanie had his attention. They did not know but we knew he was dating her undercover. He didn't think we knew but we did. My dad would bring me to school and he would tell him that it was ok to paddle my behind. Back in the day we had does wooden paddle and the teacher didn't mind using it. I had one teacher and he would always say something to me and I would punch him in the face and he glasses would fall off. Yes I was a hot mess. He always dare me to do something stupid and I did it trying to prove to my friends I was the class clown. It was good in some classes because you only go to the classes you like. I love to go to Miss Clancy she was the sewing teacher. I love to go to the cooking class. Remember gym when you played basketball. All the other things you did and enjoyed it. Christmas meant so much when I grew up yes we thought it was a Santa Clause. The Christmas tree was trim in silver angel hair that would make you but itch if you get to close to it. My mother favorite dish for Christmas was this thing that look like a dog laying in pot. One day I was looking for something to eat and I pull the top off the pot and run and told my mother it is a dog in the pot she told me it was a coon. Growing into a teenager had the best parent you would ever had. I know one thing if you are thinking about things you want to do. I would like to be honest I was more of a follower I see something I want to do the same. My friends and I would wait upon her mother go to work at night take her coats in the day time she worked as a school teacher. I would hide under the bed and she didn't know I was even in her house. So when the clock strike 10.00 we would grab the coat and walk up to 16th street. Teen town was where the hang out we would go dancing. Sit around and chat. Laugh and just have fun. It order for you to join in with the vice lords. You would have to be jump in so they would put you against the wall and beat you up But they didn't do us like that they pretended to jump us in. Living in a disciple terrority it mean if you live on one side of the road that mean you can not cross over to the other side. How about me living right on the side of the disciples and being a vice lord. I had a friend that tried to cross over in the disciple on his birthday coming to see Linda and she told he not to come over but he got shot right in front of my house. He died on his birthday. He had just brought him some new shoes. They he was laying dead in the park. He took that chance and it cost him. That was the first murder I ever seen. I was young never went to a funeral I was so afraid to go and look at his body. Dancing in the day what they call stepping we call it the bop. The line dance we called it the bus stop. Nothing new just change the name.

The old way may could have survive a mine stone if it should have been going on today. I can remember this 7 foot man I knew him. I was going to a friend house and I was by myself. All of a sudden this 7 foot man was behind me. This friend lived on the 3rd floor close in a game way we called it back in the day. He was watching me all the time so he following me up to the house and when I knock I go no answer so on my way down he tried to grab me and rape me but I broke a loose from him and jump the flight of stairs but in that they you were young and if something happen you did whatever it took to save yourself. When I go to the bottom of the stairs he begin to chase me. I ran like hell. When I go to trip street in the middle of the street I kick my shoes off ran and ran, I can remember looking at my school this how close I was to my house. But the time I got there I thought about it I have a friend that live right there I was not about to do all that running and let this guy caught me. My friend house I jump up all those stairs and almost kick their door down. They asked me what was wrong. I told them this guy was chasing me and I could make it home. They said stay here until you think he is gone. So that is what happen on that day. I had this so called boyfriend on the same street. We were lover for a while. We would just hang out on 16th street we would go dancing and to eat at teen town. We was hanging out one day and he decided we would just go to the club house that they I was not in the move for any drama from him my feeling was changing my mind was changing I just wanted to do something different.

When I didn't want to have sex with him he would chase me home. I was running so hard and he did cross over into the disciple side of the street. I turn around he was this close to me and I fell into a deep hole that was in the park. If was crying out for help he left me in the hold thank God it was no dirt around this hold he might would have buried me alive. I heard a man walking by and I cry out to him and he said what are you doing in that hole and he pull me out. My God has been around me all my life. 16th street it was some big time gangster that if you mess up you will have to pay the price. This guy has tried to rape me when I told him no. I went the next day to talk to the chief of the gang and they found that guy and it was sad what had happen but he should have known better. The beat this guy so bad I never went on 16th street ever again and I never saw this guy no more. Before this stuff start happen me and my friend V would wait until her mother go to work. So I would pretend I would be sleep and I would lock the door behind me and go to her house and hide under the bed until we thought her mother was leaving. Her mother was a school teacher by day and a nurse by night. To think we was something that we wasn't we would take her mother fur coat and wear them when we go on 16th street. Off we go through the night to the hide out. Next to the pool room is where we would go to dance. I was always a lover of dancing. The bop the rubber band man the bump. There was always good place to eat. We have this place across the street. They had the best double polishes. There was the taco place there was the place you can get all of you chickens wings that would make you want to lick your finger. This basement that was the hang out they have made it to a living spot. So of the gang members were living there. We had different name we have the enforcers which I was a part of the ridgeway vice lords just to name a few. We would get together with other gang and march down town to form truces. These day we live in is totally different the second killing I hear about was sad. This killing was so unnecessary. This man only wanted peace in our street. It was a bloody that day and it became a cover up. This is a day you will never forget as long as you live. Today December 4 1969 I was 14 years old as of today murders are still happening in people homes. They are going to wrong houses. This murder turn a lot of thing around believe me or not it is a lot of things like this is going on. When you think about how they went into this funeral and turn the body upside down. I was just walking across the street we you are young you are afraid to go and look at dead body people started running everyway. Now I begin to get older time to move on to something else in life. I would live my house and go to my friend D house and her mother and sister and brother D and I did a lot of things together. Sounds like we could have been best friends. Stay tuned. We started dating these two brother. T and J. Man I thought I was in love and I thought this man was in love with me. All the time he was just using me for his sex toy. I didn't care. His girlfriend lived in Mississippi and once and a while she would visit now he was in love with her. He always would say to me if you don't want to get beat up you better not come around. I was no punk them or now. We was heavy drinker and I was not afraid I was ready for whatever. You want to play with me think twice. He go just what he needed. I went on about my life after this went on for some time I move on to my next journey. Think believe after so many years people starting dying and people start moving back to there original home in Mississippi. I believe that is what happen to this guy. My friend lived around the corner we would venture off to different things. Her mother would buy the ingredients for chili and she would ask me to make it. The first time I made it they fell in love with it and almost everyday they would ask me to cook it. I love going over to my friend house because it was somewhere to go and I know we would find these to do. We night fell I would try to get home. I live a distant from her. It was the same area I grew up in almost the same spot. I just couldn't get away my childhood neighborhood. They never asked could we walk you home so I would go walking down the street all by myself they wouldn't even ask me to stay all night so I didn't have a choice but to go home in the night. Never thinking about anything happening to me I would just walk. One night I was on my way home I got about three block from their house I was now going pass my old elementary school. It was Dante elementary on polk street when I got to the alley I seen this man walking behind me I had on a long coat with a steak knife in my pocket as soon as I got ready to cross the alley this man grab me and I grab the pole. He was pulling and pulling and I was screaming and screaming to the top of my lungs. I can remember this woman looking out of the three floor window she hollow out let that girl go. And this sucker ran as fast as he could and I continue to go on my way home. The next day I was back to the same old routine how many time you get in life. I saw this guy the next day in the park. I called the police and told them what happen guess what they said it was nothing they could do. How about you getting this rapist off the street so no other women have to encounter this man. After that I went on with my life. So a couple days later walking down the street. Independent maybe 3 block for reaching home. This guy came up behind me with a gun. He said stick up and I grab the gun and I knew him because I knew his grandmother she have blue hair. He was kind of special needs person he was not playing with a full deck. He I am walking across the street because I saw the police sitting there straight in front of me and I got close to them and they pull off. I just went home. Before I did that I went back to the guy and told him to go home and I will be over there to talk to his grandmother and so that I did and she took control over what he had did. So I decided I want a new change it was my friend in 8 grade we starting hanging with my friend G. I always was loving on some good looking men. She had two brothers Daniel and I cannot remember this other brother name. Daniel was kind of cute. The other brother was dark and ugly. Daniel I like but he was marry I didn't know the other one had just gotten out of prison so he was more hard up the Daniel remember he already was marry. This ugly brother was asked to take me home so I got up and left with him I living right down the street he took me somewhere up north and all of a sudden he pulled over and trying to rape me and I start fighting him and I just out the car. As no idea where I was so he pull up and say get into the car I told him you must be crazy. So I kept on walking and this white man said to me what is the matter. I told him what had happen and I got into his car. He didn't say anything he took me all the way home if it had not been for this man I don't know how I was going to get home. He drop me off one block from my house. I was grateful. I went back over to the friend house and told them what had happen and they believe every work I said. Looking at Daniel I asked him to kiss me. He did just that but this man had lips that taste like black hot peppers. My lips burn for days never want that kiss of death again. So these to brother turn out to be the devil from hell. They both thought wrong I was not going to let that stop me. Moving on to the next chapter in my life. I move on and met some more people. Wow this was two sister. Deb and Bar. They had a lot of kids, a grandmother. She will be drunk all the time and they have a sweet mother. Deb had a boyfriend Maurice. Bar had a boyfriend Michael. These two men had them selling their bodies. One day myself and a friend Leona was over there and they asked us to go with them we had no idea what was going on. They took us to this area and let us out on these corner and now we know what was happening. They told us if we didn't what they was going to do with so this white man pick me up and I promise this man took me to his house and asked me what are you doing out here. I told him what was happen and he let me stay at his house for a while. I another. This is before people try to discredit the black and begin to plant drugs in the neighborhood. We would have this club house where we would get together and dance and we would have to pay a quarter to get in, we have cookies and plenty of Kool-aid to drink it was never any hard booze has we call it when I grew up. Growing up was really fun. I can sitting in class at Herzl elementary Mrs. Mc Calvin and looking out the window all of a sudden she said we need to have a prayer because the president just have been shot. That was a sad day and everybody went home. I can still see that blue glass on the fireplace on Douglas and Lawndale reading not what your country can do for you but what you can do for your country a statement John F. Kennedy wrote. 1968 when sitting in the window watching television Dr. Martin Luther King was killed and we had to stay in the house because the whole Roosevelt St was on fire. I wanted to be out there so bad and I know my parents was not having it. We was allowed to go out the next morning but they had called out the National Guards. All the stores was close down or burnt down it was sad, they set curfew for everybody I can remember when I first started driving a car. I was driving a cab with my friends Fannie don't know what was happening with my friend the others was already used to being on the street. I guess they was some kinds of pimps. So the next day they tried it again I was over to Leona house and he come Deb and Bar to her house and tried to force us to prostitute for these men. Leona was so scare they couldn't get us to come out so they left. After a while we stop going to their house. The last I heard of them to guys they had go kill and I don't know if they were together but it didn't make me a different. Sorry they had to go like that but I know it was not going to down like that. I remember hearing from Bar a while later and Deb had already die. They were so nice in the beginning but allow men to control them. They had to take care of those men. That didn't pay off. Let me tell you something it was a lot of these going on back in my time to. Children can go out to play. When I was born and growing up in Chicago things was more calmed you could play in the Park you could go to a neighbor house and eat with the family. You might hear somebody stole something off a clothes lines. Somebody stole somebody lawnmower. But give and take things could get a little crazy. It always going to be crazy people. People stuck together black people look out for one father. He was the one that help me learned how to drive. He was a cab stand owner. We are growing up and we begin to hit the club scene. Wow we were on Cicero Ave Joe new look lounge on cicero. Me my sister doll and Fannie we were a singing group we call ourselves the dolls sisters. We would be singing we were loved by the men. One day we got a break and we went into traveling the states. One stop was Mississippi. So we made poster to advertise who we were and we have sheet wrap around our body and we posed for the picture and we travel to Mississippi and we hung our poster up. People start coming to see us every night. When we was singing at one club we had took a break and when it was time for us to go back on stage we couldn't get a sound to come out so we tried to walk off the stage and her daddy said get back on that stage I believe if it was for us nobody was going to come see just a band. I was so hot there and we had no idea that mosquito was so bad there we go ate up so bad when we finally got home we had to see the doctor. My sister doll was really in bad shape. My sister and I went and got a job and we started working for Zenith the Television place right on Dickens and Austin. We worked there for years and they finally went out of business. We receive a lump sum of money. And we move on to other job. I remember working at panic express and we was sitting and eating lunch and all of a sudden my I heard this sound and I ran out of that lunchroom and I saw my sister hair blazing everybody sister there watching her hair on fire and I saw my coat sitting on the back of a chair it was a brown coat and I grabbed it and threw it on top of my sister head and smother it out. The ambulance came and took her away and she did live. Her recovery was a long one but she did survive. Sometimes you think you are in a great relationship you are young and it turns out to be lust. Everything that glitter is not gold or silver. What do you do when you dating and you find out it is a wife in the picture. You have to realize that you may not be the one. Maybe he will go back to his wife or maybe he will divorce her and marry you. How about you find out you and this wife has the very same first name and from the same state. Wow. When I met my children father I thought this was the love of my life. This man was tall dark and handsome the whole package. He was the disc jock in the club I party in day in and night. He nickname was slick. I knew he would be faithful because me and my friend Joann were she lived up stair over the club where my children would stay with her children while we would plug club sets. We would go to one club pay our dues. And the will come back to us and at the end of the year we should have gotten all the money. It never happen we thought we was getting free liquor but we paid for it at the end. What a good time we had. We had a lot of disc jock and all of them would play good music. That is what you call music. Poppa was another good disc jock. All of them was awesome on the turn table. Back in the day we was called classy ladies. We would dress nice we were called sophisticated ladies. We were called the west side brick houses. My partner in crime was much other than me, but I really was good friends she was my ace in the hold. We never cross each other. You talking about somebody that could drink without getting drunk man she use to drink me under the table when I got from under the table she was still going strong. If you never been drunk before the bed spin around it take a minute to get to sleep. When you wait up you have a hangover the owner he would buy food and I would cook and we would eat. Hold on to good people. I lost contact we her and now she has pass away. I think I was about 18 years old and she was in her thirty she had a couple of boyfriend I remember one guy she dated the found him in his car dead. She would have a man that make sure she had money in her pocket. People started to pass away. One day it was my birthday and they have gave a big glass of whiskey I drank a lot of that stuff and got so drunk I got on top of the bar and started dancing. Wow all can to an end. Hosea pass away first, so when that happen the club close up. My friend move in with me for a while. She left Chicago and move back to Saint Louis and I live on Congress and I was going to stay there for a while. I have a boyfriend name Prince and he was a money making machine, I remember my son got hit by a car and he had to stay in the hospital for a while and I stay there with him. He would go and work on car and bring me all this money. One day he did something that really turn my thinking around I asked him to leave my house. So I have to help him I threw him down the stairs. I threw his close behind him. I looked out the window and he was doing push up in the middle of the street. My kids father had left town with somebody else wife but the guy found his wife and brought her back to Chicago with his children and he had the nerve to call me to send him some money I didn't think so he got there the best way he could. He had the nerve to come to my house and thought everything was good I sent he on his merry way I met this guy name Carl and he was so handsome I dated him for a while Carl was there that night and he didn't even know that this fool was at my door. Really you chose to leave me and there is not coming back here. I moved on. I always wonder why people want their cake and eat it to. I mean they are marry and dating you at the same time and they think you are not going to find out. When I got with Herman I thought this was the one. We grew up together. He was in the United States Navy going to go back in. We started dating each other and one day while we was sleeping my kids does two little boys got up and went over to my mother house it was a long walk crossing dangerous streets and my mother called me and said where are you kids. She said they are over here. A few weeks had pass so he decided to go back in the Navy and I stayed behind for a minute. One day I travel to Virginia Beach Virginia to be with him. I stayed there for a week and went back to Chicago and later I had to finish School I was going for my high school diploma and going to Malcom X College at the same time. I went to high school at night and College in the day time. I had drop out of high school a while ago and one day my longtime friend we grew up together and we became next door neighbor told me about the high school and I went a completed this with a B had my diploma and one day when we was getting ready to move to Virginia cleaning out the garage at my mother house we was staying there for a while. I set my diploma and some more stuff here come some person by the time I got back to the garage this fool had took off with my stuff I tried to chase he but he got away as of this day I do not have a copy. We lived in Virginia Beach for almost two years. We have been through some stuff. This man thought the things he did was normal. Example women call your house and you sitting right there. Picking up his daughter mother from the airport the both of them tried to disrespect me like this is what life should be do what you please the devil is a liar I am not going to have it. He said I am going to see my kids and she was bringing them she came by herself. She flew all the way from South Carolina. I thought he was crazy. You don't bring your ex or your present girlfriend in another women space. He lost his mind. When we finally decided to move from Chicago and move to Oxnard Ca we go marry in February 15 1992 in Ventura Ca and we just went to the court house and not have a wedding. I went to take the civil servant text and pass after 2 tried and land a good job working for the government December 4 1989 before that I would find odd and end job I met this woman and she help me find a job at a nursing home for senior I was a dish washer and a cook. I started working at a day car and in order to get this job I had to know this scripture it was the lord is my sheppard and I shall not want this landed me this job. I was not going to be brought and a long ways from home this man didn't give me money he paid the bills. One day this lady I met told me how to get to the welfare office of the bus and I with down there and I got two check a month and food stamps and working my I was doing great. This man never knew what I was doing I would beat him home before the mailman deliver the man. I would get my check and I would send some of that money to my family in Chicago. One day we was drinking and we have got into a fight because I stood up for myself I would never back down so I took a typewriter and smash the class table into pieces he didn't believe it. I started to believe that if you can't beat them you join them I tried to find me a sugar daddy. I met this man and this man was also in the navy and he was alright he look ok but it was hard for me to fall for him I tried but this man body was scared up so bad I couldn't find myself sleeping with him yes I got into his bed and nothing could happen because of the medicine him was taking this man have lots of money he was living in a nice house he had airplanes nice car and he said to leave my husband and he will give me anything I wanted. The next morning on my way to going through the navy base gate the first person I saw was this man I could not believe this is the same man I just laid in his bed and as me and my husband was riding through he said you know this guy because they was friends both in the navy and I played it off no I don't know this man. We stayed in Oxnard for a while and then we moved to San Diego CA and when we moved we lived in Camarillo CA for a while.

????? This man did everything under the sun. When we left Virginia we move back to Chicago we move up north and we stay there for a while. He started staying out all night long and one day he lock his keys in his car and had to call me and I went to Rosa a lounge where he was listening or playing his base guitar and when I got there he was sitting with this lady fine out it was one of the friend sister I left and

waited for days for him to come home and he was gone for almost a week and when he finally showed up he thought this was what he should do whatever he please. He didn't stop there he would lay across the bed and watch porn and talk to his woman on the phone I would walk in the house and this is what he did. One day he was talking on the phone with his lover he met while out of town playing with this band. I mean everywhere this man went he would find a way to cheat. One day he came home and this same woman he move where she was he was gone for a while so I went to the bank before he could take all the money out and withdrawn but I forgot about one account and he was able to draw that out. While he was gone all that time I never heard from him I went out and brought a new car. I move out to this place on the west side and this place had rats so big I was sleeping one night and heard a loud noise and I thought somebody was breaking unto my house but it was a big rat I jump up put of my clothes and went to my mother house. I can't live in a house that has rats. I move out the same week I move in but before that happen my husband found me and I let him stay with me and I went to work and when I go home he was gone it had found everything he was looking for and he our marriage license and I thought I had hide them well. He was gone again so I made up in my mind that was it. I don't know as of today what was his motive but he been running for a long time. Sometime you have to let go but you have to hold on to God unchanging hand. I could have turn another way but it took me a while to go out on another date.

I met somebody. So much had happen nobody knows your story like you do. He decided to come back and I thought he had changed but I didn't let my guards down he said why you change the lock. I said you don't live here. He didn't he was going to live again this time he went back to his ex girlfriend until she realize this man is never going to change this man has had a triple by pass and where he is now I heard he was living with his daughter. Wow I wish him the best. I started dated this guy and this man I could feel something was not right this man was looking at 16 years old girls one night he came over and it was like he drug me and I was sound a sleep and he went into my 16 years niece room in his birthday suit nake. I didn't find out until the next day my niece thought I wouldn't believe her some she told my son and a friend. One day we went to a store and they began to talk about it and they began to tell me about what this man have done. I believe it automatically because this ugly man was weird but you know it you can never judge a book by the cover. So the next day I went to his job at burger king where he was a security guard and confronted him, he deny it but I sitting there in my car with him and I looking at this man and all of a sudden horns started coming out his head God showed me the devil was sitting right in my face. I said you can stay away from my family. I went on the website of the correctional center and I type in his brother zip code and up pop this man with this criminal background and what he had did he spent nine years in prison for assaulting a 16 year old girl in an alley. That was the end to that situation I never seen him again yes he tried to call me but not today satan. Move on with life later that year 2010 I was suppose to go to a job picnic but I stay at home. The night before I was talking with my son Deandre and he came into my room and say mother I can't breath and I didn't know what he was talking about he was on the porch and I went out there and always somebody is at my house this night it was him and one more person. We started talking he said I wish you would move from this house. He had a glow about him I gave him twenty dollors and the friend left and he came in a I saw him sitting on the couch all day the next day I was trying to call him because he never will go anywhere with letting me know where he is going. Night comes and I don't here from Shonuff and my niece and grandson went down in the basement and he was laying on the flood dead. I ran down there and I tried to wake him up but couldn't so we call the ambulance and they came and said he was deceased omg this was the hurtful pain I have ever seen. Now I had to make funeral arrangement for my baby just he was 29 years old a person with a kind heart and he and I would go to church every Sunday not seeing him on the passenger side of my car was going to be hard. So I buried him it took a while to recover from this. So I move to Michigan and I have to go somewhere and get out of this house. I can remember tell the agency I brought the house from it somebody going to die in this house or somebody die in this house he said how did you know that I didn't know that the person that sold me the house son have die in a motorcycle accident and my own son die inside this house I lived in Michigan about 3 and a half years and the water got so bad down there and it was a drive I tool every week in First time I took a month off because I thought I was going to go and open up a business. I gave this man 3500.00 so he could move to Michigan I never thought he was going to do right but he took all that money and brought drug I didn't know this man was going to buy all this drugs and lie about it. He would talk to my sister in law about what he was going to do and talk about me like a dog. Wow the things people say and do after they get your money. He came on winter night and got all his stuff and move back to Chicago it was a dream come true. I was ready for him to go. He would tell my sister he will drive my car half way back to Chicago after he kill me and my son. He was a lot of talk but no action she didn't have to tell me I hear him on the phone will I would go over to her house. People say and do a lot when you have a little money and they can get something out of you the money runs out. 2013 yes I won 20,000 dollars and every time I would come to Chicago from Michigan I would win 500.00 every time money was flooding that year but me the nice person I am was giving people money but I tell you one thing if it ever happen again I will not just give my money to everybody. One time I gave a so called friend 1300.00 dollars and gave her friend 400.00 and one day we was on our way to greater new birth and this friend gave me 200.00 and she was trying to give me back some of my money, one day she call me after years had pass. She said when I get my income taxed I am going to pay you back. I told her I wrote it off because you cannot worry about people that get money from you and they don't pay you back. Few years pass by and she passed away. I hold no grudges against people that owe me I let God fight my battle. I wish them nothing but good. I always thought it is better to give than to receive. That did not stop me from giving money away. Make sure to sow into Good ground because if you sow into stony ground you will yell no harvest. I went through and lot of things in my life after losing most of my family member and now I realize that I have nobody but my family that is still here and it make you want to get closer. I realize I am the last person standing in my family. I got myself together and I turn everything over to God and he began to work it out. I wanted to find out what my gift from him really was. I could sew, do crafts, I found myself doing a lot of writing, sermon. I started writing so much I turn it into a book. I have wrote two book and I have finish my first book. Waiting to publish. Now that I know what my gift is that God have given me. I am going to finish these books. Never a loud people to dictate to you what you can or cannot do. This thing is something you are built to do and nobody and beat you from being you. Now since I am older and growing into the person God wants me to be. I found me. Knowing that faith is a little thing you grow into. Nothing can separate me from the love of God. God is my peace he is the peace maker. He is my righteousness he is my counselor he is my savior. He took this imperfect person looking to be perfect one day and that might be when I make my last breathe but until God say well done I will continue to do what he call me to me You have to finish what you started. You are your worst enemy and your own best friend. I been working since 1972 at the age of 18 years old and at the age of 65 years old I am still working. I always wanted to be a hard worker. It is time to hang up my uniform and work on things I love to do. I join the gospel truth ministries. And I am still a member. I have learn so much from being under the leadership. My Pastors. Where the word works. I have to come to reality it is time to live the prime of my life. With all the murders, rapist, series killing, I want to spend a lot of time praying. You realize that we need more prayer and we need to pray harder. One accord and obedience is the key to change. You know when you are called by God to do a work and you cannot let anybody stop you it is not all preaching it is about working the work of him that sent you many are called but few is chosen. When you been to the first degree and you reach your peak of storms you know it is time to do what he call you to do and go full force. To love him is to obey him with question. I want to live the rest of my life living for Christ. Called to the ministry over 30 years ago have to ensure a lot of heart aches and pain have to understand what it take to be chosen by God. Growing up in Chicago I am been a lot of religion Catholic, Lutheran, apostolic Baptist sanctified all he religion took me to a journey to where I have landed to a relationship with God. I never knew I would end up where I am now under a great man of God where there in a connection in the spirit the anointing of God has led me to non demination a personal relation with the holy ghost where I feel I am o tolerated on mess. Negitive can not live with me but you know you can't get away some people don't know how negative is alive. He is so amazing how God is covering you and chosing you for such a time as this. This corona virus has kill a lot of people has effected a lot of people. Some people still don't believe in God but I pray for them this is how you know reason while you know you are called by God. Things matter in my life it is not how bad a person is or been all of us can change but it is left up to the person if that is what they want in their life. You cannot pour Jesus on anybody, because I do believe 33 tornado touch down in the south killing a lot of people. Snowing in Chicago on April 17 2020. Using people for the mark of the beast. The book of revelation is coming alive and people still don't get it. People still think it is science. How do science make the sun shine? Snow, rain, make grass grow. Created baby where did people come from. I pray to all the reader and writer when God tell you to do something don't listen to people. You will get to the place where he wants you. We watch people daily they still standing on the corner still killing still in group. No social distant. This what I believe that it is not going to be the same thing that happen. You have the flu, you have the aids nothing is going to stop some people but death. The bible say in hell you shall lift up your eyes. I do feel as if it is a personal relationship with. You have to know where I am coming from. It is personal with me not just because I been through a lot in my life but I can find peace in the midst of it all. Many are called but few in chosen. You have to know when you been chosen by him. Never let people turn you away from what you believe and trust in. Some people are so selfish and don't give a hill of bean about you if they this you are not good enough to tie their shoe. Some people if you don't have nothing to give them watch does dogs. You become the worst person that ever live. They become your enemy they don't talk to you anymore. Don't tell them you can up on some money and he they come but you have to shake them off. Yes looking over all these years and remembering your life and how far God have brought you and to see a lot of people passing away and some are murder to see all these thing and you are still here why not do what you were put down here to do. You cannot allow people to hold you back you are your own person and you move by call command. Love yourself and love other but with a long handle spoon learn how to listen to the voice of God is there a reason why I am still on this earth. What is the reason why I have accomplish what I was put here to do. God does not need me but I do need him. How good he is to me. Not ever been so great or good. So thankful. Been talk about might even been spit on. But I still here to tell my story. Who can tell your story greater that yourself. The life you live belong to you. You know your ups and downs inside and out mind control is everything I learn to listen to God and let him direct me into what he call me to do. From gang member to the minster. Tell me what God can't do. He know what you will be doing at all time you may not know but he does.

You cannot fool he. He knows all and he see all. What it is meant to go from midnight to daylight is to go from some of the darkness place it was different when I was coming up we had love for one another we played together we eat together. How about that girl that climb tree and did all boy thing and still grow up to be a beautiful young lady never even known that a person that wanted to change the identity and it never cross my mind to judge somebody that is God job. Growing up in the fifty we played game jump ropes and they say you cannot think about the pass the time we live in now parents want to drink with their kids and get high with their kids let their kids stay out all time of the day I remember the street light better not be gone off before you have that body in that house your mother better not asked where you were. When going up you hustle just to have money in your pocket mother and father did not have a lot to give some if you took can and bottle to store back in the day 10 cent would but a pack of cigarette 5 cents would but a candy bar. I have my favorite candy. Milkyway candy bar. Kool cigarettes dill pickle when I got older came up with an idea and I said I might as well sale candy on my parents front porch always wanted to have my own business even in my early years. Every way you go you try to hustle and have money in your pocket you didn't have to take somebody life to have something. I can't remember people trying to destroy other family to get what they want you might have had some break in I don't remember a lot of bad thing. It was not perfect but times have changed so much. What would we do to make it a better place or a better time to let people live a long life some many people have lost their life to soon. What ever happen to let live. What ever happen to let loved. The grave yard are full of people that lot their lives. Love ones gone to soon. Sometimes I sit at my desk and think a lot I looks at some of my co workers never will understand them. I have to stay focus on me. After through life my heart was away on going to church. I guess born it tell you when you are going to come into this world. The dash in the middle tell you all the things you are going to do. I am not going to talk about death because I am still living. Life I find out in my older days when I chose to live by myself not to have a man in my life just a lot of Jesus. Not that man have made my life a living hell. I chose to be for God and I found out that sometime enough is enough. One of the reason relationship probably don't last is be that some of us sex will keep him. Don't believe that. It works two ways. It is a different that separates love for lust. When the fire burn out you can still stay together because you were in love. When God join you together like no man put you under. When a man fined a wife he finds a good thing and obtain favor. I threw a couple of scriptures for free. I decided to live best life. I seek God for what it is he want me to do. It has been over twenty years since I accepted my call into the ministry. Until you come into the full knowledge of God and until you have that personal relationship a one on one encounter with God you can understand why it is hard. You have to endure hardship you have to go through some storms you have to hit some bumps. You have to lose some love ones you have cry you have to laugh you have to pray. It is so much you have to do. It take a strong person to get through life but without God being first in your life. If God be for you who can be against. Iron sharpen iron. My character is a little different. I have seen the way I operated when it comes down to the way people treat me. I always and still do think you can be kind to people but sharpen your discernment because you learned that people are people and you can help them always but that don't change who they are. Some people really value you as a friend and some id a begger and some say can I borrow this and that and they know they is not going to pay you back and they look at you and think I owe this person and I can't pay them back and maybe I wasn't going to pay them back between two people I leaned money two both are dead now. People should own up to what they say. Now you have to be aware of what you allow in your personal space. People lie and the will tell you any to get what they want. You don't have to stay in that frame of mind. Life goes on with god in First place. People don't believe that you can goes through life without getting burnt. I am a living witness. 65 and still going strong get ready to retire after 31 years of Government and it has been a curse and a blessing. Working with different kinds of people it has been a rocky end. New people begin to come in people talk about you but with going off and venting it to me almost all my career to understand it was not necessary. It was myself have to realize the power of God that help you make it through. My Pastor along with some friend. Robin said with love and kindness have I drawn them. I learned through that is to not so much love the people that miss treat me but to when it boil down to I am is to do thing is silence. Sometime is going to be broken is silence and the more you walk through the fire the stronger you get. It can take years. But if you trust God and much as you should you will be able to help people get through some people listen and some people don't but the one that listen steal your thoughts but they get some kind of way. It don't matter if they get to the point of change. I learned the hard way the soft way it was not about who you think you are and how people look down on you as long as God know who I am and whom I am I am somebody is his eye sight God is the author and finisher of my father he is the first the last the great I am. The peace that surpasses all understanding if you stand with god you can ride this wave and reach the surface of life that god design for you. You are wonderfully made and there is nobody like you. If you have a twin and you look just them it is going be something different about one you. Even if somebody get something for me it is not always meant for me to move with that thing if it meant for somebody else it is a thing to be able to realize we help each other. Believe me I try to be the most friendly person try to me a godly as I can but not perfect. Playing like I am the most holy person in the world is crazy. I am not going to fool you or myself it might take a life time to get it right. All have sinned and fallen short of his glory. Never will I let somebody tell me any different live your life like it is golden. Nobody is going to live forever. Born of a women received by a natural father. Birthday dash in between mean I have live my life and did everything I could whether it was good bad or ugly my life has to continue until God say well done I am so glad that God is a forgiving God and he holds the key to life and death until he say it time to come on up a little higher there is why I stand.

China Black

Printed in the United States
by Baker & Taylor Publisher Services